GRANDFATHER
REMEMBERS

GRANDFATHER REMEMBERS

Memories for My Grandchild

Conceived and Written by JUDITH LEVY
Designed and Illustrated by JUDY PELIKAN

A Welcome Book

Harper & Row, Publishers, New York

Cambridge, Hagerstown, Philadelphia, San Francisco, London
Mexico City, São Paulo, Singapore, Sydney

1817

Edited by TIMOTHY GRAY
Text copyright ©1986 by Judith Levy
Illustrations copyright ©1986 by Pelikan Inc.
Printed and bound in Japan

For information, address:
Harper & Row, Publishers
10 East 53rd Street
New York, New York 10022
ISBN: 0-06-015561-2

Published simultaneously in Canada by Fitzhenry and Whiteside, Limited, Toronto

I'd like to share some memories,
And I'll do the best I can,
So you'll get to know your Grandfather
As a boy and as a man.

With love for _____

From _____

Date _____

TABLE OF CONTENTS

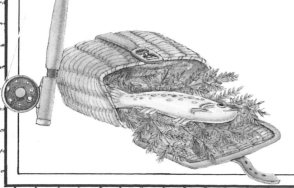

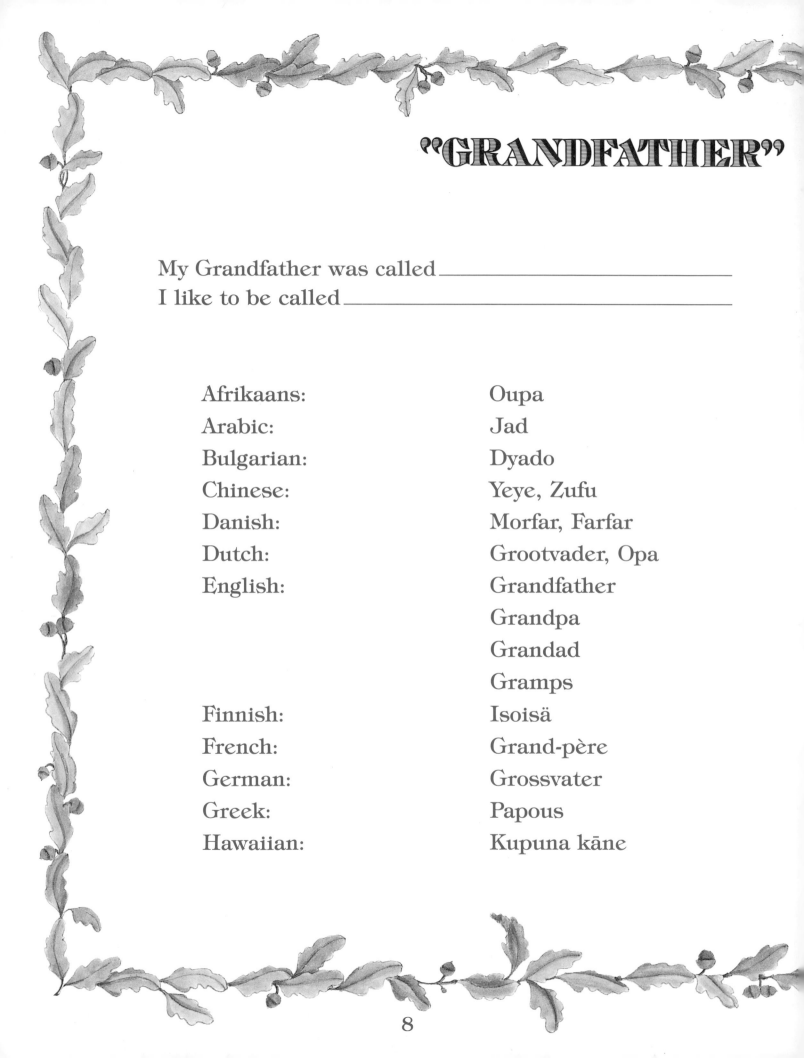

"GRANDFATHER"

My Grandfather was called _____

I like to be called _____

Afrikaans:	Oupa
Arabic:	Jad
Bulgarian:	Dyado
Chinese:	Yeye, Zufu
Danish:	Morfar, Farfar
Dutch:	Grootvader, Opa
English:	Grandfather
	Grandpa
	Grandad
	Gramps
Finnish:	Isoisä
French:	Grand-père
German:	Grossvater
Greek:	Papous
Hawaiian:	Kupuna kāne

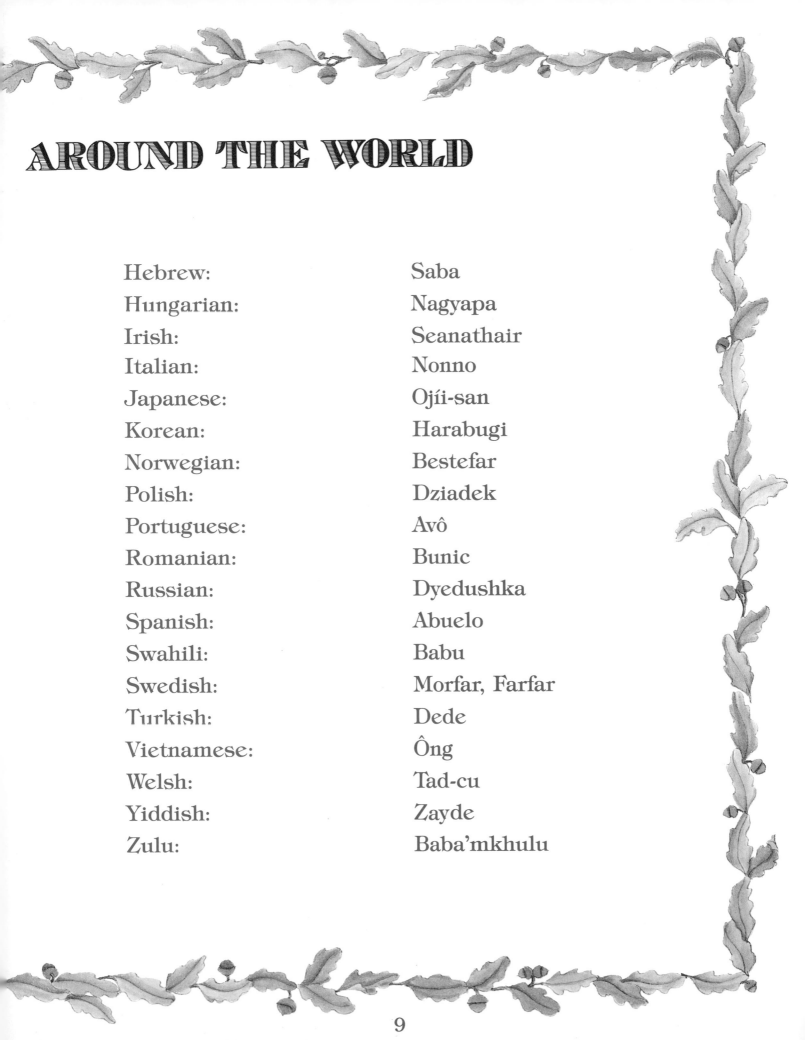

AROUND THE WORLD

Hebrew:	Saba
Hungarian:	Nagyapa
Irish:	Seanathair
Italian:	Nonno
Japanese:	Ojíi-san
Korean:	Harabugi
Norwegian:	Bestefar
Polish:	Dziadek
Portuguese:	Avô
Romanian:	Bunic
Russian:	Dyedushka
Spanish:	Abuelo
Swahili:	Babu
Swedish:	Morfar, Farfar
Turkish:	Dede
Vietnamese:	Ông
Welsh:	Tad-cu
Yiddish:	Zayde
Zulu:	Baba'mkhulu

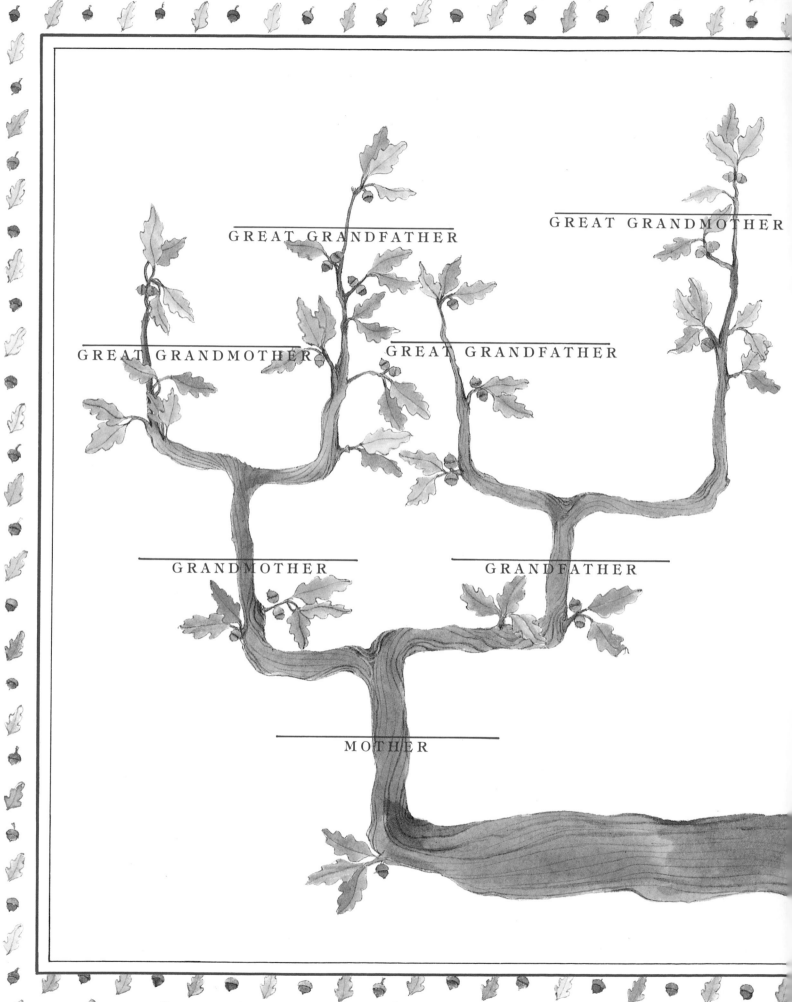

GREAT GRANDFATHER

GREAT GRANDMOTHER

GREAT GRANDMOTHER

GREAT GRANDFATHER

GRANDMOTHER

GRANDFATHER

MOTHER

OUR FAMILY TREE

Growing taller every day
With branches very dear,
Our tree has truly blossomed
Now that you are here.

GREAT GRANDFATHER

GREAT GRANDMOTHER

GREAT GRANDFATHER

GREAT GRANDMOTHER

GRANDFATHER

GRANDMOTHER

FATHER

GRANDCHILD

MY GRANDPARENTS

My Mother's family

My Grandfather's name _____

My Grandmother's name _____

My Grandfather's heritage _____

My Grandmother's heritage _____

They settled in _____

My Grandfather earned his living _____

_____

_____

_____

My Mother was born on _____

My Father's family

My Grandfather's name _____

My Grandmother's name _____

My Grandfather's heritage _____

My Grandmother's heritage _____

They settled in _____

My Grandfather earned his living _____

_____

_____

_____

My Father was born on _____

Photo of
My Parents

MY PARENTS

My folks were very special;
I think of them with pride.
I loved my Mom and Dad,
And they were always on my side.

My Father's full name _____

My Mother's maiden name _____

My parents met

    How _____

_____

_____

    When _____

    Where _____

They were married

    Date _____

    Place _____

My Father earned his living _____

_____

Photo of Me

As a Baby

I WAS BORN

About the day that I was born
I don't know very much.
But here are just some simple facts:
The date, my weight, and such.

I was born

When _____

Where _____

I was named _____

I was given that name because _____

_____

_____

My weight was _____

I was told I resembled _____

_____

My Brothers' and Sisters' names _____

_____

_____

_____

_____

Photo of Me
As a Boy

AS A BOY

Life's many highways
Stretched before my eyes.
Where my path would lead
Would come as a surprise.

My family lived _____

_____

My room was _____

_____

Our neighborhood was special because _____

_____

My jobs around the house were _____

_____

A hardship my family had to overcome was _____

_____

As a student I _____

_____

My ambition was _____

_____

My parents taught me to value _____

_____

What I loved about my Father was _____

_____

What I loved about my Mother was _____

_____

I was taught to drive by _____

The first car I drove was _____

The first car I owned was _____

The car I dreamed of having was _____

What I worried most about in those years was _____

_____

My happiest memory of those years is _____

_____

_____

As a Boy "My Favorite . . ."

Game or hobby_____ Spectator sport_____
Team_____ Player_____
Participation sport_____
Book_____ Comic book_____
Singer_____ Song_____
Radio program_____ Movie_____
Actor_____ Actress_____
Super hero_____ Subject in school_____
Friend_____ Pet_____
Holiday_____ Food_____

In my spare time, I_____
_____
_____

I spent my summers_____
_____
_____

My parents were very strict about_____
_____

I once got into hot water for_____
_____

I got my spending money by_____
_____

I used it for_____

22

AS A YOUNG MAN

I was graduated from _____ date _____

After I finished school, I _____

_____

On weekends, I _____

_____

A major news event was _____

_____

It affected my life because _____

_____

I served my country by _____

_____

What I remember most about those years is _____

_____

My favorite political figure was _____

I felt that way because _____

_____

My concerns about the future were _____

_____

I felt optimistic about _____

_____

_____

A postage stamp cost _____

A movie cost _____

A gallon of gas cost _____

I met your Grandmother at _____

Her full name was _____

Her birthday _____

Her heritage _____

On our first date, we _____

_____

I liked her because _____

_____

She said she liked me because _____

_____

When we dated, we liked to go _____

_____

We were sentimental about _____

_____

_____

As I look back, I think as a young man I _____

_____

_____

MY ENGAGEMENT

There's a very special feeling
When loving hearts meet,
And I knew if Grandmother married me,
My life would be complete.

Our courtship lasted _____

My parents thought she was _____

_____

Her parents thought I was _____

_____

I proposed at _____

_____

When I asked Grandmother to marry me, I said _____

_____

_____

And she said _____

_____

We became engaged on _____

Our Wedding Photo

MY WEDDING DAY

Your Grandmother looked so lovely,
I was proud she was my own,
The dearest wife in all the world
A man has ever known.

Grandmother and I were married

    Date _____

    Time _____

    Place _____

I wore _____

_____

I thought your Grandmother looked _____

_____

My best man was _____

Your Grandmother and I celebrated our wedding day by

_____

_____

_____

What I remember most about my wedding day is _____

_____

_____

After we were married we traveled to _____

_____

Photo of
Your Grandmother and Me

MY FIRST YEAR OF MARRIAGE

When Grandmother and I were first married, we lived in

_____

_____

My job at that time was _____

I earned _____

Around the house, I liked to _____

_____

The car I drove then was _____

When we took trips, we liked to _____

_____

As a husband, I tried to be _____

My fondest memory of your Grandmother in those years is
the time _____

_____

_____

My favorite homecooked meal was _____

_____

Your Grandmother and I looked forward to _____

_____

_____

_____

_____

_____

MY OCCUPATION

Caring for my family,
With rent and food and clothes,
I needed a good occupation,
And here's the one I chose.

My first full-time job was _____

_____

I was responsible for _____

_____

The job I liked the most was _____

_____

I liked it because _____

_____

_____

The most important promotion I ever had was _____
_____
_____

The most challenging job I ever had was _____
_____
_____

The best career decision I ever made was _____
_____
_____

Photo of Me
and My Baby

I'M A FATHER

"Hello, we had a baby!"
So many folks to call.
Everyone was so excited
And I felt ten feet tall.

Your parent was born
　　When _____
　　Where _____
　　We lived at _____
Full name _____
We chose that name because _____
_____
Sometimes we used the nickname _____
Color of eyes _____ Hair _____
My first reaction on seeing my baby was _____
_____
My baby's personality was _____
I still laugh when I think about the time _____
_____
_____
As a father, I tried to be _____
Brothers' and Sisters' names _____
_____

33

Photo of My Child

MY CHILD GROWING UP

The first day of school
Came around so fast;
Before I blinked my eyes,
The early years had passed.

Schools attended were_____

_____

_____

Best subject in school was_____

Showed talent in_____

_____

Ambition was_____

_____

Hobbies were_____

_____

When we spent time together, we liked to_____

_____

_____

What I remember most about those childhood years is___

_____

_____

MY CHILD'S TEENAGE YEARS

The teenage years were hectic,
With many a sleepless night.
Though Grandmother and I shook our heads,
It all turned out all right.

Favorite type of music was _____

Major interests were _____

_____

Household chores were _____

_____

Spare time was spent _____

_____

_____

Dating began at the age of _____

I set a curfew of _____

I was strict about _____

_____

Photo of My Child

As a Teenager

Once got into hot water for _____

_____

_____

I was very proud that _____

_____

_____

What I remember most about those teenage years is _____

_____

_____

_____

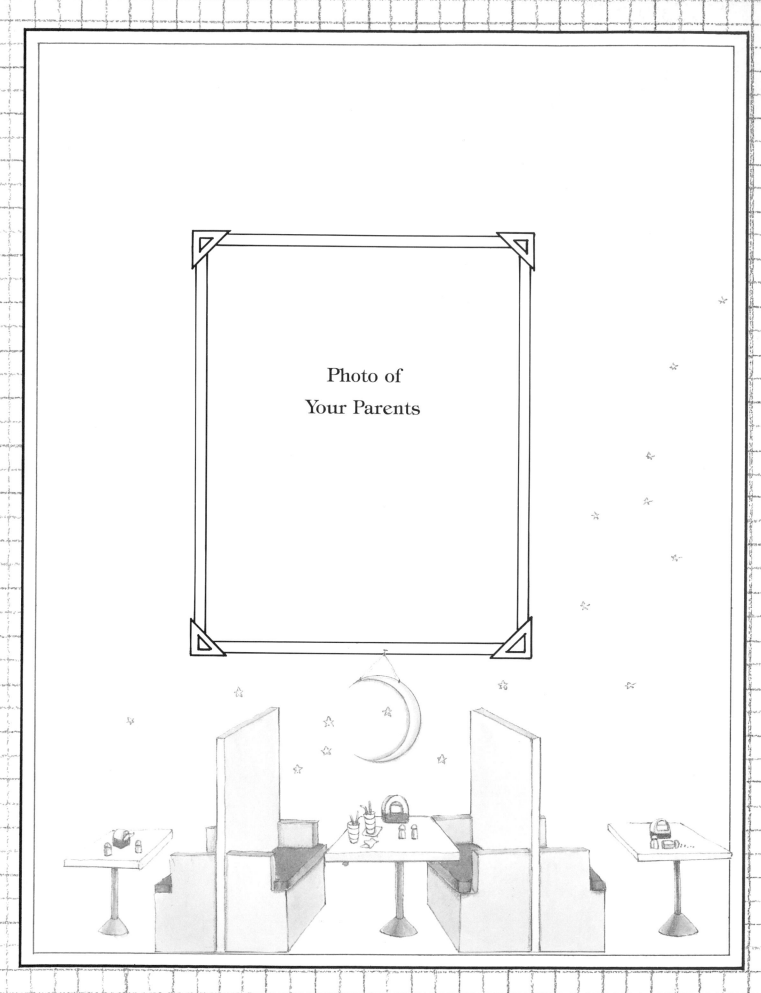

Photo of
Your Parents

YOUR PARENTS

They met
How _____

_____

_____

_____

When _____
Where _____

_____

They were married
Date _____
Place _____

A Baby Photo
of My Grandchild

YOUR BIRTH

So many feelings
I've kept deep inside.
But when you were born
I just burst with pride.

You were born

    When _____

    Where _____

When I first heard the news, I _____

_____

When I first saw you, I _____

_____

I thought you resembled _____

_____

When I brag about you, I always say _____

_____

_____

_____

_____

_____

_____

The first holiday you shared with us was_____

_____

We always recall the time_____

_____

_____

We always laugh about_____

_____

_____

When it comes to carving a turkey, I_____

_____

FAMILY GETS TOGETHER

Remembrances of our family
Always warm my heart.
They'll keep you ever near to me
At times when we're apart.

We still remember when you_____

_____

_____

I'm happy that we all_____

_____

_____

I think our family is special because_____

_____

_____

_____

OUR FAMILY

I consider it to be
Really quite a plus
That people so nice
Are related to us.

Name _____

Relationship _____

Photo

Name _____

Relationship _____

Photo

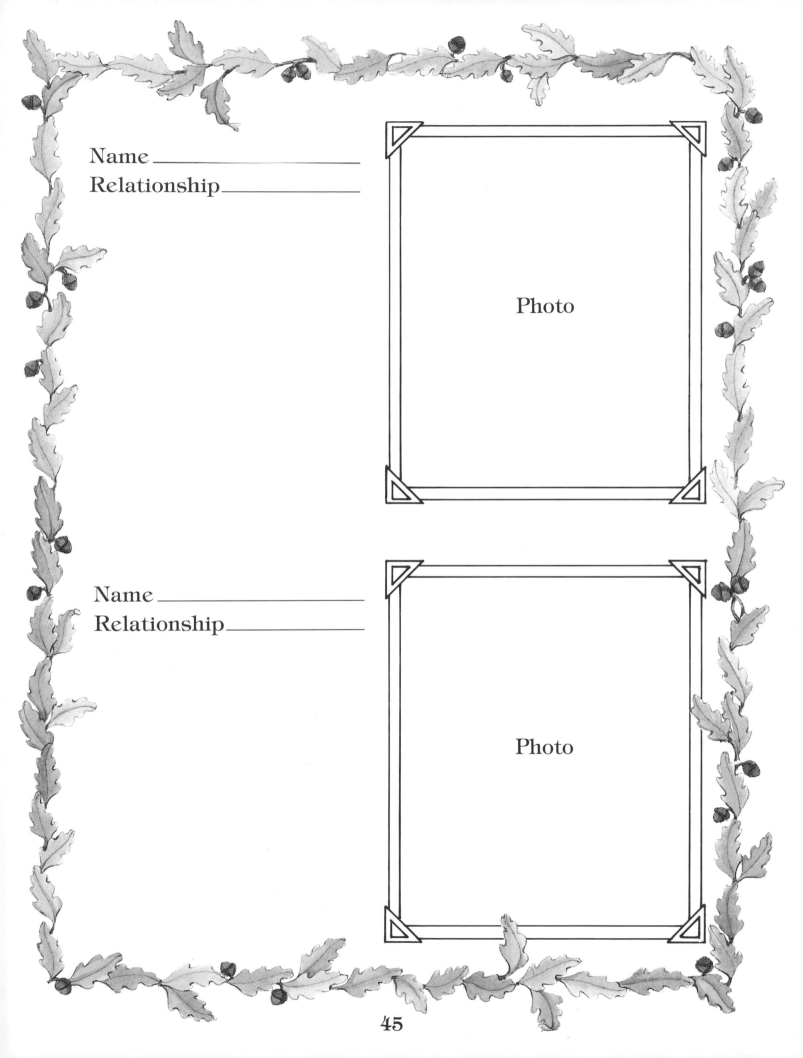

Name

Relationship

Photo

Name

Relationship

Photo

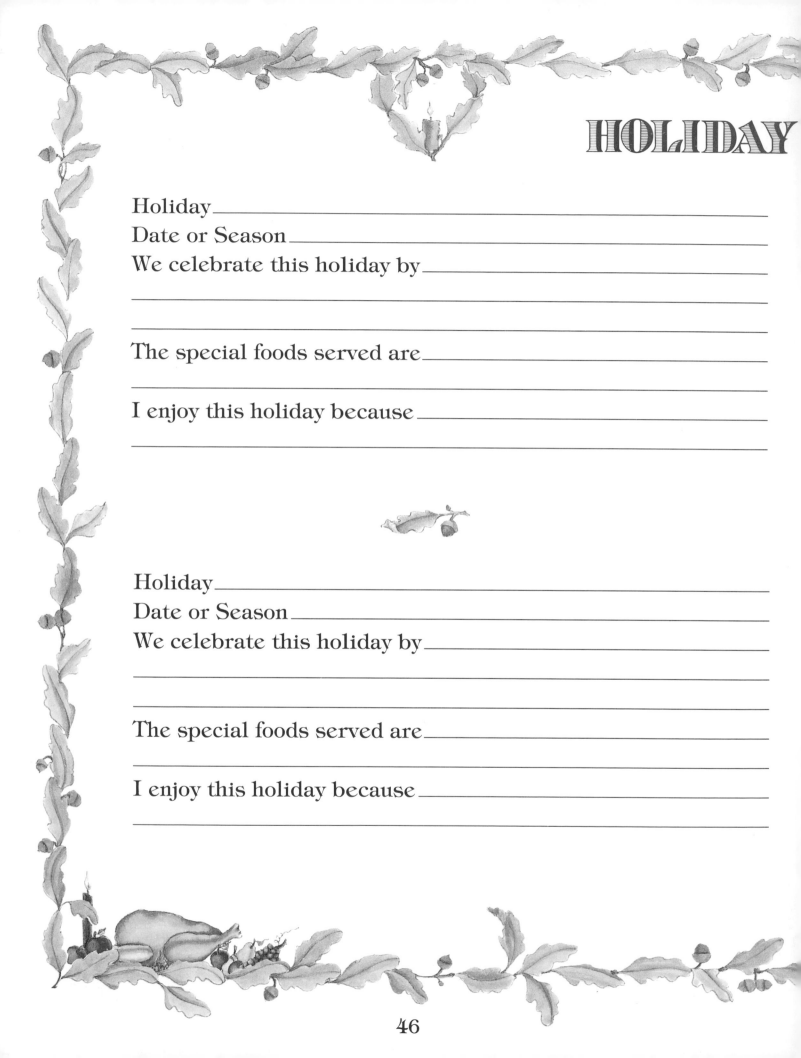

HOLIDAY

Holiday _____

Date or Season _____

We celebrate this holiday by _____

_____

_____

The special foods served are _____

_____

I enjoy this holiday because _____

_____

Holiday _____

Date or Season _____

We celebrate this holiday by _____

_____

_____

The special foods served are _____

_____

I enjoy this holiday because _____

_____

TRADITIONS

Holiday _____

Date or Season _____

We celebrate this holiday by _____

_____

_____

The special foods served are _____

_____

I enjoy this holiday because _____

_____

Holiday _____

Date or Season _____

We celebrate this holiday by _____

_____

_____

The special foods served are _____

_____

I enjoy this holiday because _____

_____

TRAVEL

My first trip was to _____

I went with _____

My age then was _____

My first trip on a plane was to _____

My most adventurous trip was to _____

_____

What I remember most about that trip is _____

_____

_____

The funniest thing that ever happened to me on a trip was _____

_____

_____

Places in this country I have visited_____

_____

Foreign countries I have visited_____

_____

Places I would still love to see are_____

_____

My favorite vacation spot in the whole world is_____

I like it because_____

_____

_____

HOW THE WORLD HAS CHANGED SINCE I WAS A BOY

They invented _____

_____

They succeeded in preventing _____

_____

When man landed on the moon, I _____

_____

A time-saver my father never had is _____

_____

A man's responsibilities are different today because_____

_____

_____

A woman's responsibilities are different today because_____

_____

_____

Movies today are different because_____

_____

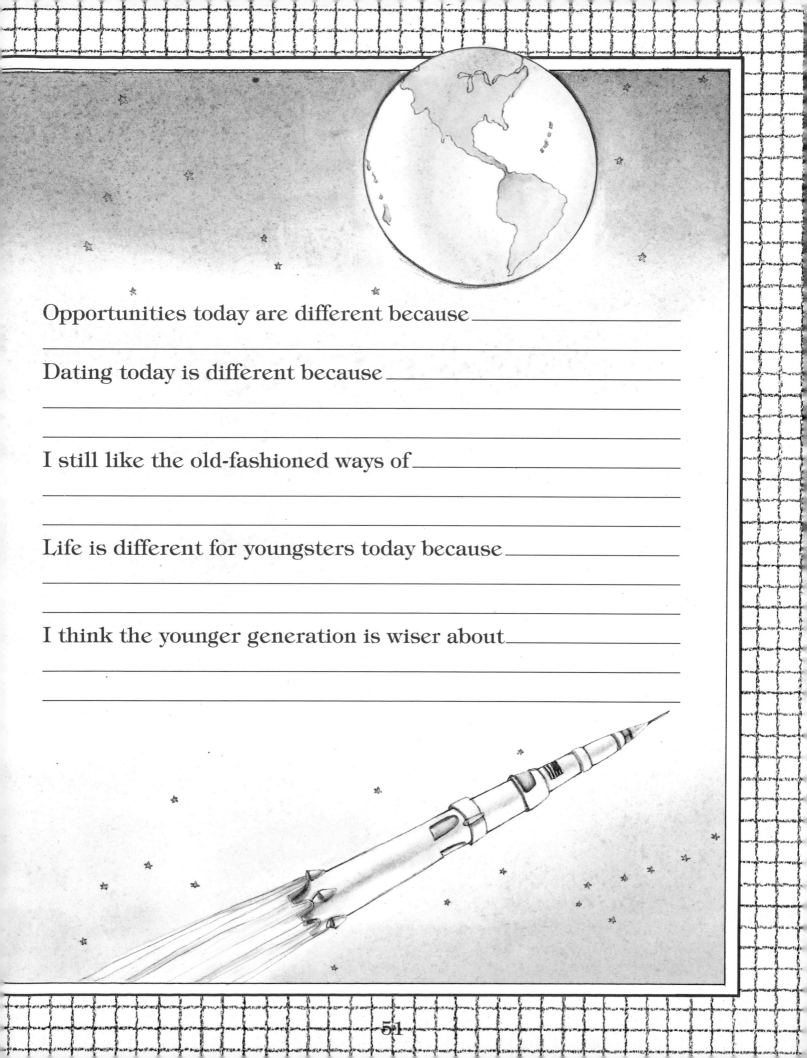

Opportunities today are different because _____
_____

Dating today is different because _____
_____
_____

I still like the old-fashioned ways of _____
_____
_____

Life is different for youngsters today because _____
_____
_____

I think the younger generation is wiser about _____
_____
_____

RISKS AND MONEY

You'll never know what might have been
Unless you give it your best shot.
Sometimes you'll win, sometimes you'll lose,
But give it everything you've got.

A risk I took that worked was _____
_____
_____

One that failed was _____
_____
_____

The lesson I learned from that was _____
_____

VENTURES

The best money deal I ever made was _____
_____
_____

When it comes to borrowing money, I think _____
_____

When it comes to lending money, I think _____
_____

When it comes to spending money, I think _____
_____

When it comes to saving money, I think _____
_____

If you go into a deal with someone, my advice is _____
_____

My attitude about money in general is _____
_____
_____

A LITTLE KNOW-HOW

Something I could give you
Might be lost; however,
Something I could teach you
Will keep us close forever.

I would enjoy teaching you _____

_____

I first learned it when I was _____

I was taught by _____

I enjoy it because _____

_____

_____

_____

_____

MY FEELINGS

I want to share these thoughts,
So you can clearly see
Just what counts the most
To a guy like me.

A simple statement that sums up my attitude about life is

_____

_____

My deepest values are _____

_____

A philosophy I've always lived by is _____

_____

My religious beliefs are _____

_____

I used to feel very strongly about _____
_____

I've changed my mind and now I think _____
_____

In my day, men weren't supposed to show emotion; today
_____

I think it's manly to _____
_____

My definition of a "good guy" is _____
_____

Men I admire are _____
Women I admire are _____
People who influenced me the most were _____
_____

They influenced me because _____
_____
_____
_____

56

I was always proud of the time I _____
_____
_____

I always regretted I didn't _____
_____

My "pet peeve" is _____
_____

As a friend, I try to _____
_____
_____

If I had my life to live over, I'd _____
_____

One of the best things about growing older is _____
_____

The most precious thing in the world to me is _____
_____

TODAY, MY FAVORITE

Hobby _____

Spectator sport _____

Team _____

Player _____

Exercise _____

Book _____

Author _____

Newspaper _____

Newscaster _____

Television program _____

Song _____

Movie _____

Actor _____

Actress _____

Car _____

Place to live _____

Holiday _____

Snack food _____

Joke _____

_____

_____

I wasn't always perfect;
I got grounded for a few.
But my Grandfather always loved me,
And I'll always love you.

Photo of
Me Today

Photo
of Grandmother

GRANDMOTHER WOULD WANT YOU TO KNOW

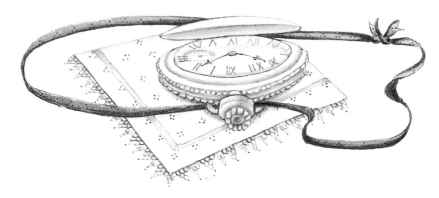

THE FUTURE

I wish you so much happiness
In everything you do,
And a grandchild who's wonderful
And loved, just like you.

My hope for the future is _____

_____

_____

_____

_____

_____

_____

_____

If you tell your grandchildren one thing about me, I'd like
it to be _____

_____

_____

_____

_____

_____

_____

_____

_____

_____

_____

_____